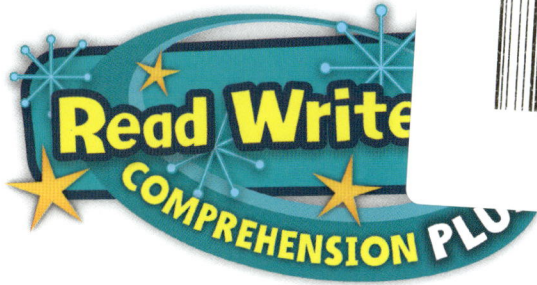

# Read Write COMPREHENSION PLUS

# Pupils' Book 5

**Janey Pursglove and Charlotte Raby**

**Series developed by Ruth Miskin**

## OXFORD
UNIVERSITY PRESS

# OXFORD
UNIVERSITY PRESS

Great Clarendon Street, Oxford OX2 6DP
is a department of the University of Oxford.
It furthers the University's objective of excellence in research, scholarship,
and education by publishing worldwide.

First published 2010

ISBN: 978-0-19-846990-2

3 5 7 9 10 8 6 4

**Acknowledgements**

Cover illustration by: Andrew Painter; Cover photo by: Vince Clements/Shutterstock.

The publisher would like to thank the following for permission to reproduce photographs:

**p14t**: Photography by Hardwick Studios/www.hardwickstudios.com; **p14b**: Bigstock; **p25**: MEN syndication; **p34t**: Kokhanchikov/Shutterstock; **p34b**: Hemis/Alamy; **p45t**: With kind permission of Anthony Horowitz; **p45b**: MGM/Everett/Rex Features; **p63t**: Heinz Schmidbauer/A1PIX Ltd.; **p63b**: James P. Blair/National Geographic/Getty Images.

Illustrations by: Maria Cristina Pritelli: **p46, p48, p51**; Russ Daff: **p56t, p57, p58**; Andres Martinez Ricci: **p6–8, p10–11**; Paul McCaffrey: **p9, p49, p52–54** Andrew Painter: Contents, **p15–21, p23**; Mike Phillips: **p36–37, p41**; Martin Sanders: **p35r**; Victor Tavares: **p27, p29b**; David Semple: **p4–5, p22, p24, p26, p29t, p30–33, p35t, p39, p43–44, p55, p56b, p59–61, p64**; Lazlo Veres: **p13, p47, p50**.

Printed by KHL in Singapore

Paper used in the production of this book is a natural, recyclable product made
from wood grown in sustainable forests. The manufacturing process conforms
to the environmental regulations of the country of origin.

# Contents

# Unit 1 Prometheus and Pandora

## READING

### ① Word power 1 TTYP

Story 1 and Story 2 use these different ways to say the same thing.

★ *by mistake   accidentally*

★ *cross   angry   outraged   furious   livid*

★ *trick   fool*

★ *for ever   evermore   without end*

★ *attractive   beautiful*

**Take turns to tell your partner you are really angry with them, choosing a different word each time. Add lots of expression!**

For example:
"I am *furious* with you!"
"I am *outraged* by your
terrible behaviour!"

## ❷ Read a story version 3 🗣 TTYP

**Discuss the questions below with your partner.**

**A.** What would you say to Zeus if you met him?

**B.** Do you think that Prometheus deserved his punishment? Why/why not?

**C.** Did you want Pandora to open the box? Why/why not?

**D.** What did you think was going to be in the box?

## Challenge

Use the thesaurus tool on your computer to find more synonyms. You could start with alternatives for words used in the story, such as 'cold' and 'mystery'. Then find out what the word 'thesaurus' means. Record what you have found out in your Daily log.

## ❸ Word power 2 🗣 TTYP

**Partner 1 read the word and its meaning.**
**Partner 2 read the sentence containing the word.**

★ **eternity** – without end
This gift is yours to keep for ever – for all *eternity*!

★ **bestowed upon** – given to
One of the medals *bestowed upon* the soldier was for bravery.

★ **potent** – strong
The witch's spell was very *potent* and all the good fairies together couldn't undo it!

★ **gargantuan** – enormous
My breakfast was *gargantuan* but I'm still hungry!

★ **distraught** – very upset
Grandma was *distraught* when she realised she had been robbed.

★ **exquisite** – incredibly beautiful and perfect
That wonderful, sparkling diamond ring is *exquisite*.

★ **appeased** – soothed, calmed
The man was *appeased* once I agreed to pay for the damage I'd caused to his greenhouse.

Partner 2 read the phrase with lots of expression!

Partner 1 read its meaning.

| Special phrase | Meaning |
| --- | --- |
| *Release us from our ceaseless toil.* | Set us free from our endless work. |
| *The magnitude of your punishment will match my fury!* | The size of your punishment will be equal to my anger. |
| *For what is power without compassion?* | What is power without feelings for others? |
| *Let us rejoice in the life that we have.* | Let us be happy with the life we have. |
| *It was as if the sky's brightest and warmest sunbeam fell like drops of golden liquid onto his skin.* | He felt very happy. |

Now choose your favourite special phrase. Tell your partner why you like it.

### Challenge

Find out the difference between a **simile** and a **metaphor**. Think of a **simile** to describe 'the sky's brightest and warmest sunbeam' and write it in your daily log. Can you turn it into a metaphor?

## ⑤ Who's the most important? TTYP

Zeus?

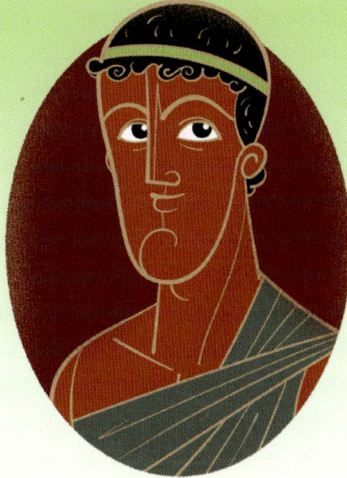

Prometheus?

Pandora?

**Who do you think is the most important character in the whole story and why? Discuss with your partner.**

## ⑥ What if not...? TTYP

**Discuss these What if not...? questions.**

**A.** What if not *powerful*? What if Zeus was *weak*?

**B.** What if not *brave*? What if Prometheus had been *cowardly*?

**C.** What if not *beautiful*? What if Pandora had been *plain*?

**D.** What if not *curious*? What if Pandora was *unconcerned* by what was in the box?

### Challenge

Zeus is the Greek name given to the king of the gods. Can you find out what his Roman name was?

Partner 1s: one of you is Zeus – the other one is his supporter.

Partner 2s: one of you is Prometheus – the other is his supporter.

Role-play the point in the story where Zeus is about to punish Prometheus. Use the prompts below to help you.

**Prometheus:** I don't deserve this punishment. I have always…

**Zeus:** Ha! You also enjoy not doing as you are told! You have…

**Prometheus:** Making the human was an accident. I didn't…

**Zeus:** If you disobey me, the king of the gods, you…

**Prometheus:** You are just jealous because…

**Zeus:** Jealous! Why? I have…

**Discuss with your partner:**

★ Did the role-play change your point of view about Zeus or Prometheus?

★ Which character do you feel most sympathy for? Why?

### Challenge

In the story, it says that Prometheus was chained to the rock for eternity, but after 30,000 years he was rescued. Research who rescued him and how they did it.

# WRITING

## ① Build a sentence

**Write a sentence starting with the word 'faltering'.**

**Think about the following questions:**

**A.** Where might someone move and act in a *faltering* manner?

**B.** Who might this be?

**C.** How would they be moving?

## ② Tell a story
TTYP

**Re-read the story so far.**

Faltering, the woman shivered as she stepped into the empty, abandoned house. The dusty hallway was full of cobwebs and a mouse scurried across the floor from beneath a crumpled newspaper.

"What am I doing here?" she whispered to herself, clutching her raincoat across her hunched body.

In the orange glow of a street light shining through a broken window, she saw four doors.

Spotting the only door that was open, she edged towards one of the rooms. At that exact moment, a dark shape was moving about on the other side of the door...

**Now take turns to make up and tell each other the next bit of the story.**

### Challenge

Write a paragraph with the dark shape as the narrator. The dark shape would be telling the reader about the events from its point of view. What does it hear/smell/see? What does it think might have entered the abandoned house? What is it going to do?

Take turns to read each section of Story 3 from your printout.
Discuss how well the human told his story.
Use the guide questions below to help you.

**A.** Which words or phrases did you like or dislike?

**B.** Was there anything that could have been added?

**C.** Was there anything that should have been left out?

**D.** Which sentences made you feel sorry for the human?

**E.** Which parts made you see why the human was grateful/sad?

**F.** What reasons did the human give for feeling like this?

### Challenge

Look in the library or on the Internet for other stories from different cultures about the beginning of life on earth. They are often called 'creation stories'. Read one or two of the stories you find and record the titles and where you found them in your Daily log.

**Partner 1: Read Pandora's words to your partner with lots of expression!**

*It started to drive me mad, not knowing the secret of the box.*

**Partner 2: Read Pandora's words to your partner with even more expression!**

**Use the prompts below to help you build up the sentence:**

★ Think of synonyms for the word 'mad', e.g. *insane, crazy, out of my mind.*

★ Change the opening of the sentence, e.g. *I tried not to think about it but...*

★ Use an adjective to describe the box, e.g. *...the secret of the mysterious box.*

★ Add some information, e.g. *not knowing the secret of the box but hearing the mysterious voices coming from it.*

**Say your sentence out loud to your partner before writing it down. Make changes to it until you are really happy with it.**

## Challenge

Write a short script of Pandora and her husband discussing what might be in the box and whether they should open it or not.

# Unit 1 Instructions

## READING and WRITING

### ① Word power TTYP

Partner 1 read the word and its meaning.
Partner 2 read the sentence containing the word.

★ **instructions** – explanation, advice, information
I need you to follow my *instructions* very carefully when making the box.

★ **procedure** – method, process, steps to be taken
Follow this *procedure* otherwise the recipe will not work!

★ **sequence** – order or organisation of something
The *sequence* of these instructions must be followed exactly.

★ **time connectives** – words to show the sequence of the
instructions, e.g. *first... next... then... after that...*
*First* mix the sugar and the eggs, *then* add the milk.

### ② Instructional texts TTYP

Texts A, B, C and D on the next page are parts of different types of
instructions. With your partner match the texts to the possible target
readers below.

★ Some texts might have more than one target reader.

★ Some of the target readers might not match any of the texts.

| 1 A teenager | 2 A children's TV presenter | 3 A grandparent |

| 4 A doctor | 5 A young child | 6 An adult who has bought a piece of furniture to assemble |

| 7 A shop owner | 8 A carpenter | 9 A market stall holder |

**A**

8 x wooden panels
4 x packs of screws (different sizes marked A – D)
2 x metal support rods
1 x tube of glue

**Method:**

★ Find pack A and check it has 16 screws (if any are missing, please call our helpline 00000 11 22 33).

★ Place panel X on top of metal support rods Y and Z. Use 2 screws from pack A to secure panel in place using a standard or electric screwdriver.

**B**

4. Then cut two holes for eyes in your cardboard mask. You will need very sharp scissors so ask a grown-up to help you.

5. Now get a red felt pen or some paint and draw a big, round nose.

6. Next, draw a very large smiley mouth underneath the nose.

7. Finally, glue all the pieces of pink and yellow wool to the top of your mask to look like hair.

**C**

D. *Make sure you have time left to decorate your wooden toy box. You could stick a transfer on the side or perhaps use up leftover paint to put the child's name on it.*

E. *Don't forget to use non-toxic paint!*

F. *When displaying the boxes, put some toys inside but make sure customers know they are not included in the price!*

**D** **How to Stay Fit and Healthy**

✓ Cut down on crisps and chocolate. Eat more fruit – it is much healthier and helps prevent spots!

✓ Do some exercise at weekends. Don't just play on your computer!

✓ Stale sweat causes bacteria which may smell. Have a shower and use a deodorant every day and after exercise.

✓ Watching TV can be relaxing but not late at night. Switch the TV off at least an hour before you go to bed and get a good night's sleep.

## Challenge

Write the beginning of the instructions for text B. You can change the numbering if you need to. Remember who your target reader is!

## 3 Ice cream recipe

**TTYP**

**With your partner, look in your Anthology for the instructions 'Have a go at... Chocolate Chip Ice Cream'.**

**Find examples of:**

★ text in boxes or bubbles

★ different fonts

★ different sizes of text

★ pictures

★ shading behind text

★ information that is not part of the instructions on making ice cream. These features make the recipe *interesting to read* and *exciting to look at*.

**Now discuss the questions below.**

★ How helpful is the extra information?

★ How helpful is the presentation and layout of the recipe?

★ What score out of 5 would you give for the overall presentation?

### Challenge

Find out at least three more fascinating facts about ice cream. Make an information sheet and use interesting ways to present the information.

# Unit 2  Bling!

## READING

### ❶ Understanding a character  TTYP

Discuss the questions below with your partner.

**A.** What would you wish for if *you* were Billy?

**B.** What would you wish for if you were given the chance?

**C.** Do you think Billy will be happier with his new friends?

**Make a prediction about how Billy's new power will make him feel and write it in your Daily log.**

> ### Challenge
>
> People are often given wishes in fairy tales. Find another example of a magical creature granting wishes in a story. Did the wish work out well?

### ❷ Images  TTYP

Find these phrases in the story in your Anthology and discuss what images they create for you.

| | |
|---|---|
| heavy with luxury | glinted with the heavenly glow of gold |
| glow of satisfaction | gleaming like gold |
| glittering wrist | gleaming with the terrible beauty |

> ### Challenge
>
> Use a thesaurus to find synonyms for *glow*, *glint*, *glitter* and *gleam*.
>
> Then rewrite the phrases in Activity 2 above using some of the synonyms instead. Put a circle around the synonyms that you prefer.

Discuss which synonyms for *walked* you might use to describe Billy in these different situations. Think of some verbs to add to your Power words in your Daily log.

Before his wish came true.

Billy approaches the cool boys for the first time.

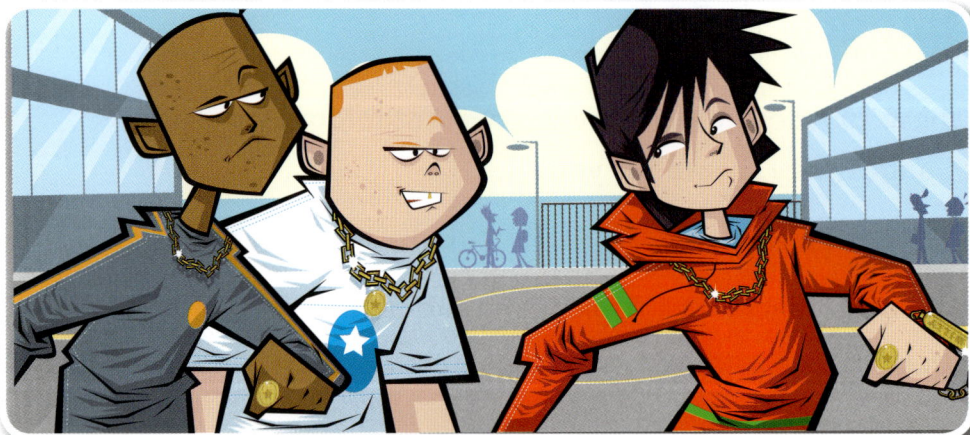

Billy was Top Dog now.

## Challenge

Make a collection of interesting movement verbs from one of the books you have been reading. Choose five fantastic ones and try them out as part of a description of a character.

## 4 What if not...? TTYP

**Discuss these What if not...? questions:**

★ What if not *'a loser'*? What if Billy had been *popular*?

★ What if not *'bling'*? What if *pets* were cool?

★ What if not *a gold-maker*? What if Billy had asked to *live in a mansion*?

★ What if not *Billy's cat*? What if Goji was *the neighbour's cat*?

## 5 Hotseating: warm up TTYP

**Discuss the questions below with your partner.**

**A.** What do we know about Billy at the beginning of the story?

**B.** How would he like his life to change?

**C.** What is very important to him?

**D.** What do we know about Billy by the end of the story?

**E.** What would he like to change?

**F.** What are the consequences of him asking for the gold-maker?

### Challenge

Add to your story map to show how Billy changes. You could use colours to represent his emotions and map out the key settings of the story. Some settings are not closely described, for example where Billy is jumped by the big boys – you might want to create additional details for your map.

# WRITING

## 1 Build a sentence TTYP

Write a sentence to describe Goji.

★ Try to make her seem cold and lifeless.

★ Now add a clause to compare Goji the statue to Goji the living cat.

## 2 Tell a story TTYP

The text below imagines what Billy might be thinking about his dilemma. Take turns to make up and tell each other the next bit of the story.

Billy gazed at Goji who was now a cold, golden statue and imagined how it would be to hold her warm, purring body again. He remembered her calm, comforting presence and the way she used to be his most prized friend.

Billy thought about the Chimichanga and its clever, thoughtful eyes as it gave him his choice. He wondered at the wisdom of this magical being and how his choices would make him think carefully about what he valued most.

With a sinking dread Billy remembered how it used to be, before the wish and the golden cushion. Even thinking about the loneliness he used to feel in the playground was enough to make him shudder. He felt the smallness of being a loser again. There was so much to lose. If he gave up the golden cushion he would fall from the dizzy heights of being Top Dog. He would become a worm again: a nobody or even worse.

Billy's eyes fell on Goji and he searched her golden frozen face. Could he give her up? Would he be able to face his new friends without the power of the golden cushion? He stared and stared, holding the weight of her life in his hands. He knew what he had to do.

*Text by Charlotte Raby*

## 3 Build a story ending 2 TTYP

**Take turns to read each section of the diary on your printout.**

**Discuss how well Billy told his version of the event. Use the guide questions below to help you.**

**A.** What makes the discovery of the Chimichanga powerful?

**B.** Identify the information used in the planning. Was anything altered? If so, how?

**C.** What new information did you learn about Billy?

**D.** How is Billy's diary different from the story?

**E.** What else could have been added to make the account better?

Partner 1: give all the reasons why Billy should give up the gold-maker.
Partner 2: talk about the consequences of doing this for Billy.
Then swap!
Use these ideas to help you.

What should I tell Mum about Goji?

Without the gold-maker I'll be a worm again.

If I keep Goji as a statue I will have killed her.

What if someone finds the gold-maker?

**Partner 1: Read Billy's words to your partner with lots of expression!**

*I begged the Chimichanga to return Goji to life, but it shook its head sadly and said it wasn't as easy as that.*

**Partner 2: Read Billy's words to your partner with even more expression!**

**Use the prompts below to help you build up the sentence.**

**A.** Think of synonyms for the word *sadly*, e.g.

*miserably, sorrowfully, unhappily, despondently*

**B.** Change the opening of the sentence, e.g.

*As I grasped Goji in my hands I begged…*

**C.** Use an adjectival phrase to describe Goji, e.g.

*my lifeless friend*

**D.** Add some information, e.g. *I begged Chimichanga with tears in my eyes.*

**Say your sentence out loud to your partner before writing it down. Make changes to it until you are really happy with it.**

## Challenge

Imagine you are Goji. How would you persuade Billy to bring you back to life? Write a short paragraph to try to persuade Billy that you are more valuable than the gold-maker.

## ⑥ Write a story 3

Use the composition prompts below to write your diary entry.
Think about the following:

★ Is it written in the first person (I, me) and the past tense?

★ Is the style chatty and engaging?

★ Are the facts straight and in order?

★ Does it say how Billy felt at key points in the narrative?

### Top Tips!

**A.** Vary the beginning of your sentences – don't always start with 'I...'.

**B.** Give personal details to make the events and setting seem real.

**C.** Tell the reader how you feel. Identify your real emotions: 'I shouted but that was because I was scared.'

**D.** Make sure the reader knows how hard it was to make your final decision.

### Challenge

This story is based on another story about a king called Midas who, like Billy, had the power to change normal objects into gold. In the story, the god Pan challenges the god Apollo to a musical contest. Find out what happens to King Midas as the result of this contest.

## READING and WRITING

### I Points of view
TTYP

**Take turns to read aloud a section of the article below.**

**A.** Discuss which of the words or phrases give away the reporter's point of view that Billy should be worried about his safety.

**B.** Write the most powerful pejorative words or phrases in your Daily log.

## Schoolboy with Super Powers?

A strange phenomenon has occurred at Dove Street Primary that has mystified and troubled parents and teachers alike. The amazing appearance of 24-carat gold jewellery on many Year 6 pupils has been dubbed the 'Dove Street Gold Rush' and has led to some children fearing for their safety as gangs of youths hang around the school grounds hoping for easy pickings.

## Golden Billy

The boy at the centre of this row is Billy Midas (10) known to his friends as the 'King of Bling'. Incredibly, eyewitnesses have reported that Billy takes metal watches and jewellery from his chums and then returns them changed into 24-carat gold. One of Billy's buddies Calum (10) told this reporter, "I didn't believe it at first but he really did change my silver chain into gold and it wasn't a new chain, it definitely was my old one changed into gold. He's the best mate ever."

## Fears for Billy

Billy Midas refused to comment on these extraordinary claims and is constantly protected by two 'bodyguards' leading many to think that he too fears for his safety. Whether Billy is a modern-day alchemist turning metal into gold, or a clever trickster, we have yet to find out. But there is no doubt that the Dove Street Gold Rush cannot last forever.

**Partner 1 read the word and its meaning.**
**Partner 2 read the sentence below it.**

★ *chronological order* – the order in which an event happens, e.g.

*The sun rose, I got up, then I went downstairs for breakfast.*

★ *time connectives* – words to show the sequence of time, e.g.

*Today* I walked the dog. *At first* it was raining. *Afterwards* I felt a little cold so I had a cup of hot chocolate.

★ *orientation* – this is often the first sentence in a recount and is used to give vital background information. This usually includes where, when and who the recount is about, e.g.

"Tom Morley of 23 Gardens Terrace, Brighton, celebrated his enormous winnings last night."

★ *Formal/formality* – recount texts can be written with different degrees of formality, from chatty to very formal, e.g.

*Chatty:* Everyone was really pleased that Tom had won so much money. They held a huge party for him.

*Formal:* Tom Morley (45) was overwhelmed last night when friends and well-wishers held an impromptu party to celebrate his vast winnings.

## Challenge

Alchemy is an ancient science. Some people used to believe that it must be possible to change metals into gold. These were often called wizards.

Research alchemy. You could look into alchemists in fiction (such as Merlin) or investigate alchemy's roots as an ancient science that goes back to the Greeks.

Take turns to read the recount 'Teenage Hero' below, sentence by sentence, with your partner. Discuss how it is different to the full newspaper recount.

## Teenage Hero

*Conor McGrath is a real hero. He saved a young family from a burning house and now may be given a bravery award. The 14-year-old saw the family was in trouble and shouted to their mother to drop the two children out of the window so he could catch them. He said, "It was one of those things you do – you just act."*

### Challenge

Have a look at some more news recounts written for children and compare them to a current news story in a paper. How does the recount change for the different audiences?

## READING

### ❶ Introducing the poem 3 TTYP

**Discuss the questions below with your partner.**

**A.** Is the poem funny or serious?

**B.** Do you think the writer likes cities?

**C.** Which line do you like the sound of most of all?

### Challenge

What can you find out about the poet Robert Louis Stevenson?

Note what you have found in your Daily log or make a fact sheet about him.

### ❷ Word power 2 TTYP

**Partner 1 read the word/phrase and its meaning.**
**Partner 2 read the sentence containing the word.**

★ *gusts* – blasts of air, draught

Great *gusts* of hot air poured from the cooker.

★ *split their sides* and *creased themselves* – burst with laughter, laughed hysterically

They *split their sides* when I fell off my chair!
The audience *creased themselves* as they watched the clown.

★ *gloated* – made the most of (in a mean way), enjoyed, wallowed in

He *gloated* when his enemy got into trouble.

★ *boasted* – showed off

"Every princess wants to marry me, of course!" *boasted* the handsome prince.

**Surprise your family – try to use each word at least twice this week.**

Partner 2 read the phrase with lots of expression!
Partner 1 read the poetic feature that the phrase shows.

| Special phrase from the poem 'Last Night, I Saw The City Breathing' | Poetic feature |
|---|---|
| *Last night, I saw the city breathing...* <br> *Last night, I saw the city laughing...* <br> *Last night, I saw the city dancing...* | Repetition |
| *And the trees* <br> *in the breeze...* | Rhyme |
| *Snaking Avenue smacked her lips,* <br> *And swallowed seven roundabouts!* | Alliteration |
| *And the wind,* <br> *Like a cat,* <br> *Snoozed in the nooks of roofs.* | Simile and rhythm |

TTYP  **Now choose your favourite special phrase. Tell your partner why you like it.**

## Challenge

Think of an extra stanza (verse) for the poem 'Last Night, I Saw The City Breathing' that starts with the line:

'Last night, I saw the city *dreaming*.'
What would the city be dreaming about?

Write your extra stanza in your Daily log.

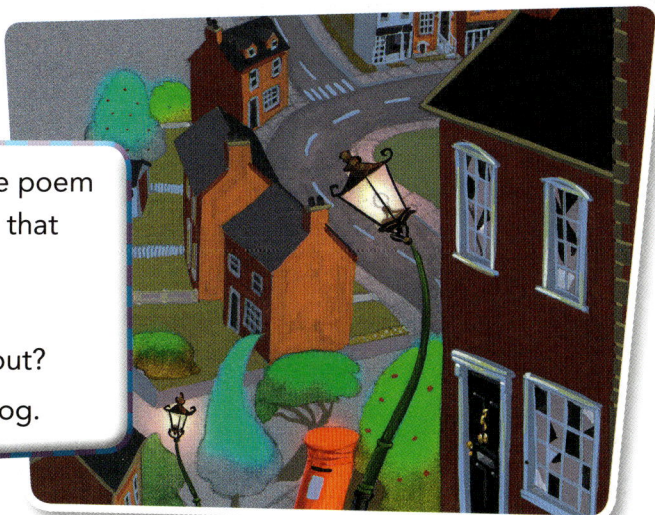

## 4 Personification TTYP

With your partner, match the non-human object to the actions in the poem 'Last Night, I Saw The City Breathing'. Check your answers by looking at the poem in your Anthology pages 32–33.

| Non-human object (noun) | Human actions (verb) |
|---|---|
| Snaking Avenue | night-dreamed |
| trees | put on a show |
| roads | boasted |
| trains | wiggled their hips |
| takeaways | got the giggles |
| street lamps | smacked her lips, and swallowed seven roundabouts! |

### Challenge

Turn personification on its head – think about what object you would be at different times of the day or week, e.g. in the morning, at bedtime, on a school day, at the weekend, or on holiday. Make a list poem from your ideas.

## 5 Dramatic reconstruction

In groups of four, choose a stanza from 'Last Night, I Saw The City Breathing' that you would like to perform.

You need to bring the words on the page to life! Think about using:

★ facial expressions

★ body movements

★ sound effects

★ pauses

★ different speeds

★ different volumes

★ freeze-frames to show an image or an emotion

**Discuss in your group:**

★  In what way has performing part of the poem changed the pictures in your mind created by the words?

## Challenge

Choose your favourite line from the poem 'Goodnight Stroud' (in your Anthology page 31) and learn it by heart. See how many more lines you can remember – learn a line a day!

# WRITING

## ① What if not...? TTYP

**Discuss these What if not...? questions.**

**A.** What if not *last night*? What if it were *this morning*?

**B.** What if not *a city*? What if it were *the countryside*?

**C.** What if not *like a cat*? What if the simile for the wind (lines 28–30) was *a lion*?

## ② Build an image

**Write a line starting with the words 'cracked windows'.**

**A.** Where are the cracked windows?

**B.** How might the broken glass be falling? Do you want to use a simile?

**C.** What might breaking glass sound like?

**D.** What might the cracks look like?

## Challenge

Cut-up poetry! These words have been taken from lots of different poems about cities:

**city   building   block   carpet   ride   towers glittering   heart   roaring   humans   electric fierce   hum   wall   street**

Write them out on a piece of paper. Cut out each word. Create a new poem by arranging the words in different ways. Think about the sounds of words together and the unusual images you can make. Write the new poem in your Daily log.

## ❸ Write a poem 2

**Partner 1 read the line below to Partner 2:**

'Whiteboard scrawled with notes'

**Use the prompts below to help you develop the line.**

**A.** Think of what the writing on the board looks like. Think of a simile, e.g. Whiteboard scrawled with notes *like a trail of ink.*

**B.** Change the opening of the line, e.g.
A *trail of inky writing* scrawled on a whiteboard.

**C.** Use an adjective to describe the whiteboard.
A *shiny* whiteboard, a *scratched* whiteboard.

**D.** Think of a synonym for the word *scrawled*, e.g.
Writing *jotted* on a whiteboard.

**Say your line out loud to your partner before writing it down. Make changes to it until you are really happy with it.**

**Now work on your own to develop line 4:**

'A football boot left behind'

**Use these prompts to help you develop the line:**

**A.** Think of what the boot smells like. Think of a simile, e.g.

…s*mells like a blocked drain.*

**B.** Change the opening of the line, e.g.

*Left behind,* a football boot…

**C.** Use an adjective to describe the boots, e.g.

A *muddy* football boot…

**D.** Give the football boot a human emotion, e.g.

The *lonely* football boot…

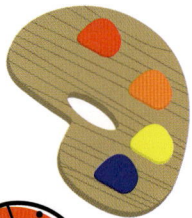

### Challenge

Haiku poems have three lines, with five syllables in the first and third lines and seven syllables in the second line. Write a Haiku about a piece of lost property left behind in a classroom.

# Unit 3 Persuasive writing

## READING AND WRITING

### ❶ Word power TTYP

Partner 1 read the word and its meaning.
Partner 2 read the sentences containing
the word.

★ **persuade** – convince, win me over,
   change my mind

   Mum tried to *persuade* me to eat more
   vegetables!

★ **fact** – truth, reality, something that can't
   be argued with

   It is a *fact* that I danced at the party.

★ **opinion** – point of view, belief,
   something that can be argued with

   In my *opinion*, I am a brilliant dancer!

★ **command** – tell someone to do
   something, demand immediate action

   I *command* you to do it now!

★ **rhetorical questions** – questions asked
   just for dramatic effect, questions that
   are not expected to be answered, e.g.
   *What on earth are...? Are we really
   expected to...? Where is the sense in...?
   What on earth do you think you are
   doing?*

## ② Audience and purpose TTYP

With your partner, match the persuasive writing texts A–D below to possible target readers (the person the text is written for).

★ Some texts might have more than one target reader.

★ Some of the target readers might not match any of the texts.

**Target readers:**

| | | | |
|---|---|---|---|
| 1 A child who is learning to read | 2 Someone who wants a job | 3 A vet | 4 A bored teenager |
| 5 A parent or carer of a child at school | 6 A pet owner | 7 The owner of a clothes shop | 8 A school caretaker |

**A**

Now, could we ask you to have a quiet word with your children about dropping litter in the school grounds? Of course, not all children are guilty of this rather disgusting habit but we are sure that every one of you will agree that it is a big problem!

If we all care about the school environment (and most of us do, don't we?) then a little chat to your children is the least you can do.

The caretaking staff have seen two rats near the boiler room and it is all because of the dreadful amount of litter. **Stop litterbugs now!**

**B**

...and I have always been keen to help other people to choose the right clothes to wear. There is nothing I don't know about fashion and so I am just the person you are looking for. Naturally you want the best person to be part of your company. I always try to be the best at whatever I do.

I am confident that if you interview me, you will find that I have all the qualities you require.

**C**

## Local library not your thing?
## Not a cool place to be seen? Think again!

Your **library** has had a make-over. Meet your mates here and experience:

- Comfy **beanbag seats** and **sofas**
- Brand new award winning **books** all waiting for you to borrow **free** of charge.
- Latest **CDs** and **DVDs** at **pocket money prices**
- Free **Internet** access.

*Join today!*

**D**

## Having a holiday? Concerned about your family pet?
# Worry no more!

Relax knowing that while you are away, your pet can play and be cared for at the **Paradise Pet Hotel**.

We have safe and secure exercise areas plus pool therapy for pooches.

All pets have a named carer and all diets are catered for.

An on-call vet is available and a web-cam lets you check on your pet anytime.

We are licensed by AHHA (Animal Holiday Home Association).

From pampered pooches and cool cats to happy hamsters and gorgeous goldfishes – we have room in our hotel and our hearts for all of them at the **Paradise Pet Hotel**.

## Challenge

Design or describe an appropriate outfit to wear at the job interview (see text B). Remember your appearance might help you to persuade the interviewer to give you the job!

## ❸ Write a persuasive text 2

Use some of the persuasive phrases below to help you to plan and create your letter or email to the football club in support of the new stadium, leisure and shopping complex.

★ Your plans are just what Denton needs! I am...

★ No one with any sense would...

★ Some of the older people of Denton don't understand that...

★ What is there for young people in Denton? Winmore is...

★ It's about time that...

★ Don't listen to...

★ Don't even think about...

### Challenge

Create a campaign slogan for the residents' group. It should be catchy, easy to remember and sum up what the campaign is about. Slogans often use rhyme or alliteration, in the same way as in poetry – try to include some in your slogan.

Think about what the campaign is trying to do and who your target audience is.

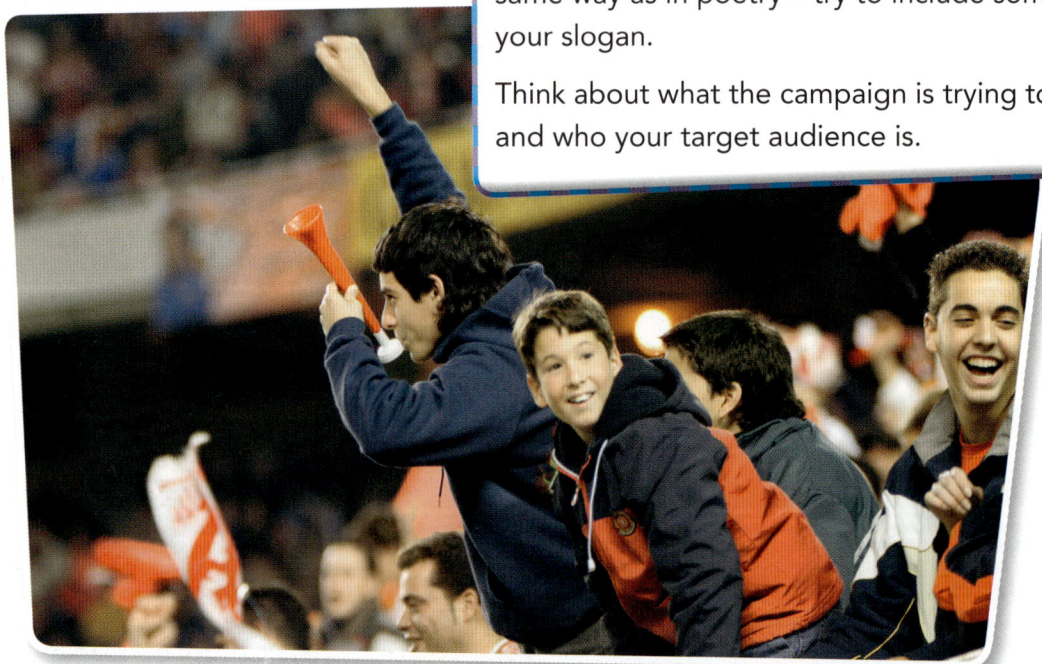

Partner 1 is *for* Winmore Stadium. Partner 2 is *against* Winmore Stadium. Read the speeches in the bubbles with lots of feeling and expression!

**Partner 1**

**Partner 2**

What's more important – a bit of grass and a few trees or a brand new footie stadium? Give me Winmore any day! Winmore! Winmore! Winmore!

How selfish! Trees are really important and don't you care about all the animals that'll just die when the park's gone?

I'm going to put my name down for a Saturday job in one of the cafés or shops when I'm old enough. I'll really need money when I'm older.

Yes well, Winmore will be able to employ people from miles away. You probably won't even get a job there and if the town shops close you'll be worse off!

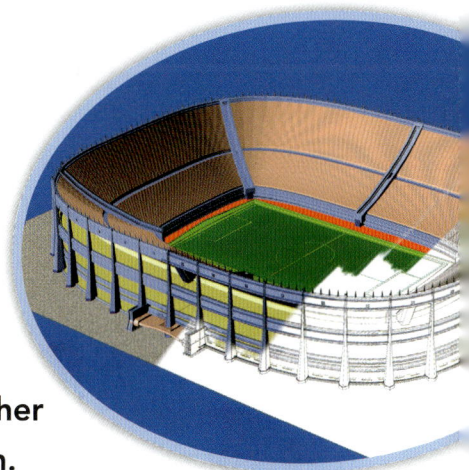

Come out of role and with your partner think of another point for and another point against Winmore Stadium.

## Challenge

Find out about your nearest football stadium. How far from the town or city centre is it? How old is it? Has it always been on that site? How much did it cost to build? If it is an old stadium, are there plans to build a new one? Create a fact file on the stadium.

# This Is NOT a Fairy Tale

## READING

### ❶ Predicting
TTYP

**Discuss the questions below with your partner.**

**A.** If Luke doesn't follow the villagers' wise advice how could he defeat all the obstacles on his way up the mountainside?

**B.** How might Jeremy Strong turn the stereotype of a princess being rescued upside down?

**C.** Do you think Luke will be successful? If so how?

**Write a short prediction about how you think this story will end.**

### Challenge

Find out more about Jeremy Strong. Visit his website and read some of his books.

### ❷ Who says?
TTYP

Take turns to read these sentences.
Discuss what the narrator thinks about Ramona.

There's a witch down there, and a bear and trolls and all sorts of horrible creatures and brambles and I might tear my dress.

Someone has actually made it to the top of the mountain and he's rather gorgeous – despite the totally untrendy clothes and strong smell of garlic.

Now take turns to read these sentences and discuss what the narrator thinks about Luke.

Down there, at the bottom of the mountain, that is where the rest of the world starts and there is so much to see and do and I am going to see it and do it and I want you to be with me.

You must make up your mind Ramona. You must overcome your own fear. I cannot do that for you.

## 3 What if not...? TTYP

Discuss these What if not...? questions.

**A.** What if not *wise*? What if Luke had been *stupid* like the rest of the villagers?

**B.** What if not *beautiful*? What if Ramona had been *plain*?

**C.** What if not *weak*? What if Ramona had been *courageous*?

**D.** What if not *achievable*? What if Luke had had to face *different obstacles* like swimming with sharks or crossing an erupting volcano?

### Challenge

Write a short piece of dialogue showing how Luke tries to persuade Ramona to follow him down the mountain.

# WRITING

## ❶ Build a sentence  TTYP

This episode could follow on from *This Is NOT a Fairy Tale*.
Take turns to read each sentence with lots of expression.

"Arrgghh!" yelled Ramona with a high-pitched scream. "How did you suddenly appear, in these woods, in front of me?"

"I crept up silently because I want to eat you," snickered the Giant Man-Eating Unicorn. "Are you a man?"

Ramona looked around and saw that she was at the edge of the woods. In fact she had hardly left the castle grounds. She could almost see the window, which she used to lean out of to gaze at the world below her. She wanted to scream but she didn't.

*Text by Charlotte Raby*

**Sentence prompts: use these ideas to help you write your sentences.**

★ Introduce Ramona with dialogue that shows how she is feeling.

★ Make Ramona introduce the unicorn by asking a question.

★ Get the unicorn to tell us about what it wants to do to Ramona in its reply.

### Challenge

Use the clues in the text to help you write a short description of the Giant Man-Eating Unicorn.

## ❷ Build an episode 3  TTYP

Take turns to read each section of the continued new episode below.

As Ramona watched Luke leave she sobbed and wished she had the courage to go with him. Although Luke was not the type of suitor she was expecting she had rather enjoyed smooching with him and hoped she could do some more. She also was rather bored with the castle. It was dull watching the world from her window and even sending paper darts over the battlements was pretty uninspiring if you never got an answer back!

She thought of all that she might see and do in the wide world and of how on earth she could continue living in a castle up a mountain, which didn't even have a telly and was very draughty and dusty. So she built up the courage to leave and meet Luke at the bottom of the mountain.

"Right," she said to herself, "I may be scared and wearing a totally inappropriate dress for mountain walking but I'm determined to give it a try."

She had hardly left the castle grounds and was walking towards the misty woods when the most terrifying sight appeared suddenly before her.

"Arrgghh!" yelled Ramona with a high-pitched scream. "How did you suddenly appear, in these woods, in front of me?"

"I crept up silently because I want to eat you," snickered the Giant Man-Eating Unicorn. "Are you a man?"

Ramona looked around and saw that she was at the edge of the woods. In fact she had hardly left the castle grounds. She could almost see the window, which she used to lean out of to gaze at the world below her. She wanted to scream but she didn't.

Instead Ramona did something she had never done before. She thought, 'I can do this. I can defeat this huge and rather nasty unicorn.'

"Are you the Giant Man-Eating Unicorn?" she asked with a quavering voice.

"I am," snorted the huge repellent oversized horse with a horn stuck on its nose.

"Well I am NOT a man," said Ramona sounding more brave than she felt, "so YOU cannot eat me!"

"Oh," said the Giant Man-Eating Unicorn sounding rather defeated, "you are right. If I eat anything other than a man I get terrible wind and awfully stinky breath. So you had better go then."

"Thank you," said Ramona feeling very pleased with herself. And then to celebrate she gave the nearest tree an almighty karate chop. To her utter surprise the tree began to wobble and then fall to the ground hitting the unwitting Giant Man-Eating Unicorn on the head and stunning him.

"I should have yelled 'timber!'" snorted Ramona to herself as she continued through the woods and down the mountain.

*Text by Charlotte Raby*

**Discuss how well it continues the original story. Use the guide questions below to help you.**

**Guide questions:**

**A.** In what way is it similar to/different from Jeremy Strong's story?

**B.** Can you identify the information used in the planning? Was anything altered? If so, how?

**C.** Could you find any jokes or puns?

**D.** Did the dialogue move the action on? If so, how?

**E.** Did anything unexpected happen?

**F.** Which words or phrases did you like?

**G.** Is there anything that could have been added? If so, what?

## Challenge

People are often given challenges in fairy tales and legends, for example Hercules and Jason in Greek myths and legends. Find a fairy tale or legend with a seemingly impossible challenge in it. How did the character succeed?

Who will Ramona meet in the forest?
Read the different character descriptions.

Hi! Some people might judge others by their appearance but I judge people by how they react to MY appearance. My dream forest encounter would be with a handsome wizard and definitely not with a beautiful princess – I really can't stand them!

Hi! I am a princess who likes nice things, handsome rescuers and pretty dresses. My ideal forest encounter would be with a fairy godmother!

**1. Waggletooth Witch**

Grrrr! I'm Black Bear, known to my friends as "Grump!" It's true that when I am hungry I can get anggggrrrry but feed me and I'm as sweet as pie. (Which I have recently discovered is delicious.) My ideal forest date would be with a fabulous cook or a huge slice of pie...

Hmpf, Glump and Bang! I am the Chief Troll and I don't have any friends because I am NASTY! Above all I am not cute or cuddly. I have very bad breath, unpleasant facial features and my idea of a good night out is to SCARE someone out of their wits. My ideal forest date would be a terrified princess, who I could sneak up on and terrify some more!

**2. Black Bear**

**3. Chief Troll**

Discuss which one you would like Ramona to meet in your episode of her story.

## 4 Write a story 2 – dialogue

When you are writing what the characters say, bear in mind the tips below.

**A.** Think of synonyms for 'said' that give clues about how the character is feeling:

*muttered, growled, squeaked, hissed, stuttered, huffed, cackled...*

**B.** Use Jeremy Strong's writing of Luke's encounters to help you. You could 'borrow' an opening sentence to start you off.

*"I'm going to put a nasty spell on you."*

*"Grrr"*

**C.** Remember to use dialogue to tell the reader what is happening:

*"Get off my hair, you pesky troll!"*

*"Look out – the tree is falling!"*

### Challenge

Get to know your character really well – use the Internet to look up photos of black bears and pictures of trolls and witches. Print some off and use them to help you describe your character better.

## 5 Write a story 3

Use the following prompts to guide you when writing your own account of Ramona's escape down the mountain.

**A.** Make sure your dialogue tells the reader what is happening or what a character is like.

**B.** Use time connectives to move the story on, e.g.
*soon after this, a little while later, straight away.*

**C.** Use adjectives to describe the new character. Re-read Jeremy Strong's descriptions to help you, e.g.
*"The trolls were short, ugly creatures with needle-sharp teeth."*

**D.** Think of unusual words or fairy tale language to describe the setting, e.g.
*the enchanted woods, a ramshackle cottage.*

### Challenge

Write a blurb for this story. Remember to make the reader really want to pick up the book and read it immediately!

# Unit 4 Biography and autobiography

## READING AND WRITING

### 1 Key features TTYP

Scan the Jeremy Strong texts in the Anthology pp.50–53 and with your partner identify examples of the key features.

| Comparison checklist | |
|---|---|
| **Biography** | **Autobiography** |
| Past tense | Past tense |
| Named person or third person (he/she) | First person (I) |
| Chronological order | Chronological order |
| Time connectives | Time connectives |
| Dates | Dates |
| Named places and people | Named places and people |
| Some additional details | Personal reflections and ideas |
| Often more formal tone | More relaxed and engaging |

### Challenge

What would be in your autobiography? Make a short plan of the key events in your life.

## ② Top Tips for taking notes

Remember these Top Tips when you write your own notes.

Only write down key words or phrases - don't copy whole chunks!
Born ~~in~~ 1956 in Stanmore, Middlesex, ~~to a~~ wealthy family

Remember to write dates and names of people and places accurately.

Read a paragraph and decide what the most important fact or idea is.

If you want to use something that someone has said, copy it down and use it as a quote. You set it out like this:
Anthony Horowitz says, "My father was a very secretive man."

### Challenge

Visit some other websites with information about Anthony Horowitz and find out about the books he has written.

**Read this biography text.**

### Anthony Horowitz

The Alex Rider books are probably Anthony Horowitz's best known works. There are eight of them and they tell the story of an ordinary 14-year-old who loses his parents and who is recruited, against his will, by MI6. But where did Anthony get his inspiration? Part of it may have come from his secretive father who kept lots of diaries in code. But the main influence was James Bond. Anthony still remembers seeing the early films when he was a prisoner at his vile school. They were the one thing in the year that he looked forward to. It was his thought that 'wouldn't it be great if James Bond was a teenager again' that led to the creation of Alex Rider.

### Challenge

Many writers had a horrid time at school. See if you can research about another writer's school horrors!

## READING

### ① Predicting
TTYP

**Discuss the questions with your partner.**

**A.** How do you think Mai-ling felt when she found out she had to slay the dragon?

**B.** What advice do you think the mysterious stranger gave Mai-ling?

**C.** How else might Mai-ling be helped with her quest?

**Now write a short prediction in your Daily log about how you think this story will end.**

### Challenge

Use the Internet to find images of Chinese mountains and volcanoes. Use them to help you imagine what Mai-ling's journey would be like.

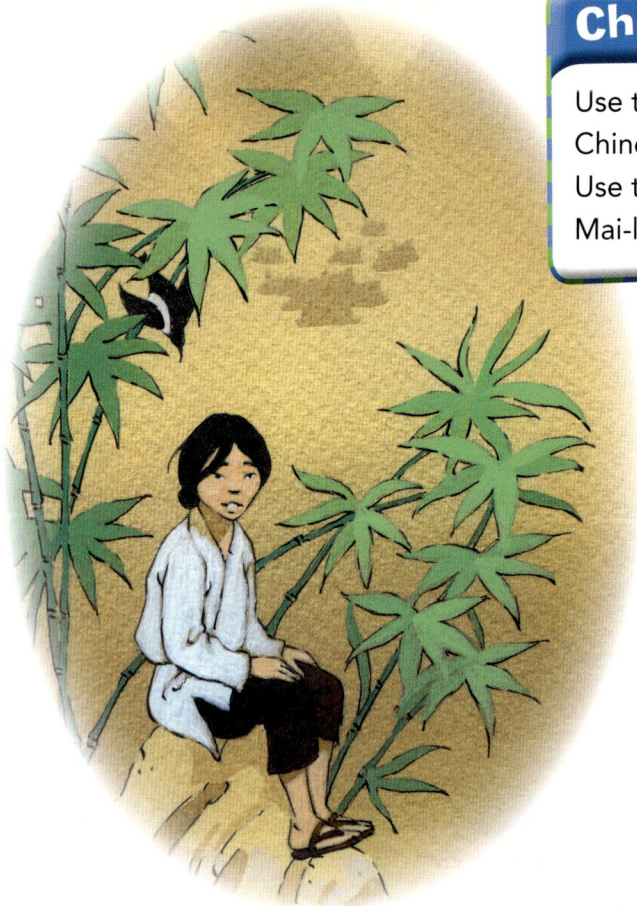

Use the questions on the Story volcano to help you draw your own version in your Daily log for the *Dragon Slayer* story.

*Story volcano*

**Dilemma** – What is the main event/action? What is the problem faced by the main character?

**Suspense** – Is there suspense? Does something go wrong?

**Build up** – How are they helped?

**Build up** – Who is chosen to solve the problem?

**Build up** – How does the problem intensify?

**Solution** – How is the problem solved? Does someone come and help? Have any of the characters changed? Has anyone learnt anything?

**Build up** – What is the problem?

**The introduction** – Who is the story about and where is it set?

## Challenge

Confucius was a famous Chinese thinker. See if you can find out more about Confucius, for example when he lived and what he believed in.

## 3 What if not...? TTYP

**Discuss these What if not...? questions.**

**A.** What if not *foolish*? What if Yen had been *wise* and asked the villagers to come up with a plan to fight the dragon with him?

**B.** What if not *lucky*? What if Mai-ling had been *unlucky* and failed to defeat the dragon?

**C.** What if not *cowardly*? What if the villagers had been *brave* and banded together to defeat the dragon?

### Challenge

Write a parting message from the shamed Elder, Yen, to the villagers.

## 4 Who says? TTYP

**Use the text to discuss the author's point of view about these characters.**

> I told you we had nothing to fear!

> Who will volunteer to kill this dragon? No one? Then I must think more deeply.

> Under the jaw between chin and throat. How can I lift your head though? How can I reach that place?

> I am only a young girl. How can I be a village Elder?

> The dragon woke. With a roar, he lifted his head and sent a burst of flame up into the sky.

> ...the village darkened beneath the shadow of the dragon's enormous scaly wings...

### Challenge

Write a few sentences in your Daily log saying who you think is the most important character in the story and why.

# WRITING

## ① Build a sentence

**Sentence prompts – use the ideas below to help you write your sentences.**

★ Start with Mai-ling hidden from the ogre's view.

★ Use a short sentence to make a startling image of the ogre.

★ Zoom in and describe a few parts of the ogre. Try to use words that revolt the reader.

★ Show Mai-ling's reaction to the ogre.

★ Decide how Mai-ling leaves the scene.

## ② Tell a story TTYP

**Take turns to read each sentence with lots of expression.**

Mai-ling stared at the ogre through the branches of her hiding place. It was vast. Its greasy, hairy body was surprisingly muscular. It sat eating a young deer, which it held easily in its hands. There was blood on the rags that covered its body. Disgusted, Mai-ling wanted to look away but she couldn't. Her eyes were drawn to the ogre's filthy hands, which mechanically stuffed meat into his huge gaping maw of a mouth. Finally, and as stealthily as a cat, she climbed down the tree to the ground and silently crept away.

### Challenge

There are ogres in legends from all over the world. Research another story with an ogre in it.

Use the Story Volcano below to help you plan your episode about Mai-ling and the villagers defeating the ogre.

*Story Volcano*

**Dilemma** – What is the main event/action? What is the problem faced by the main character?

**Suspense** – Is there suspense? Does something go wrong?

**Build up** – Who will solve the problem?

**Solution** – How is the problem solved? Does someone come and help? Have any of the characters changed? Has anyone learnt anything?

**Build up** – What is the problem?

**The introduction** – Who the story is about and where it is set.

## Challenge

Will Mai-ling face another challenge during her time as Elder of Yishan? Write a few sentences to set up the next episode of Mai-ling's troubles.

Use the composition prompts below to guide you as you write
your account.

**A.** Make sure your description tells the reader not only what a character looks
like, but how they move and what they are like.

**B.** Use time connectives to move the story on as well as to create pace and
tension, e.g. *at that moment, instantly, in a flash…*

**C.** Use a variety of sentence types. Short sentences create pace. Starting
with an emotion makes the reader think about what the character is
feeling and a startling verb or image at the beginning of a sentence
can shock the reader and make them look closer.

**D.** Try to make your story feel like it comes from China. Use some of the
words and ideas from the original story to help you.

### Challenge

Mai-ling saves her village twice!
Research other books with brave
young heroes or heroines. You
might like to start with authors such
as Cornelia Funke, Phillip Pullman,
Michael Morpurgo, Paul Stewart and
Chris Riddell, Eoin Colfer,
Susan Cooper or Anthony Horowitz.

## ❶ A field guide for ogre watchers  TTYP

Take turns to read sections of Mai-ling's field guide and discuss how the information is organised.

### A field guide for ogre watchers

**by Mai-ling**

This guide has been compiled using experience from a recent encounter with an ogre. It is intended to help anyone else with an ogre problem. Hopefully it gives ample information to defeat any ogre that is terrorising your village.

### What do ogres look like?

Despite their enormous heads ogres have small brains and are slow thinkers.

Ogres are huge. Most ogres stand the same size as a house. They are very muscular and have enormous hands, which they use to tear down anything in their way.

Ogres tend to favour a simple wooden club, if they have any weapon at all.

Ogres' feet are covered in a hardened skin, which means they can walk on even the sharpest rocks without injury.

Ogres do not wash and so are very dirty and smelly. This is useful to know, as ogres are often smelt before being seen.

### How do ogres behave?

Ogres are very aggressive. They are also quite stupid which is to the ogre watcher's advantage. Whilst travelling, ogres tend to knock down or rip up anything that is in the way. Look for the destruction, follow it and then it is likely to lead to an ogre.

### Where do ogres prefer to live?

Ogres need a constant source of food. This can be animals or humans – they are not fussy. If an ogre moves into an area it is wise to get rid of it quickly or it will eat all the wildlife, then the livestock and finally try to eat smaller humans such as children and the old. They really are a menace!

### Top Tips for people with an ogre problem

★ Ogres are very slow movers and thinkers.

★ They are also noisy so you can hear them coming.

★ Ogres sleep deeply after eating and cannot be woken.

★ Ogres can be tricked with pretty trinkets and calmed with music.

## ❷ Generic or specific? TTYP

Take turns to read the words and phrases. Discuss whether they are generic or specific. Write the generic phrases in your Daily log.

ogres    Thunder, the ogre of Yishan

some ogres    Yishan    villagers

the people of Yishan    Mai-ling

ogre watchers    you

### Challenge

What else would an ogre watcher need to know? Create an ogre watcher's kit bag with equipment they would need to watch ogres safely and successfully.

Take turns to read the information from this web page about the Knucker dragon.

DRAGONS > ENGLISH > SUSSEX > KNUCKER

# Knucker dragon

### Knucker information

The Knucker is a European dragon found mainly in woodlands, marshlands and fens throughout Europe. It has a very established habitat and breeding grounds in Sussex, where well-known 'Knucker-Holes' can be found in Lyminster, Lancing, Shoreham and Worthing. The most famous Knucker residency is at St Leonard's Forest where historical records from 1614 describe a Knucker killing livestock and terrorising the local communities. This Knucker may well have been a relative of the dragon slain by St Leonard in the sixth century in the same forest.

Knucker may well come from the Saxon word 'nicor', meaning 'water monster', which explains in part this dragon's choice of riverbanks as lairs. Unlike many European dragons it does not breathe fire but can spit acid venom, which literally liquidises its prey (this is usually rabbits and livestock). The Knucker, like a boa constrictor, tends to attack by using the coils of its serpent-like body and kills by constriction.

It is a very snake-like dragon approximately 8 metres long standing 2–3 metres high on its four short legs. It appears that the Knucker has lost its ability to fly, through evolution, and now all that remains are two useless stunted wings.

## Challenge

Find out more about ancient English dragons such as the one in St Leonard's Forest.

## 4  Write a non-chronological report

Read the text below before you write your own non-chronological report.

**The Knucker: A warning for dragon spotters!**

Unlike most dragons the Knucker does not breathe fire, rather it spits a toxic acid venom. This venom has the power to liquidise living matter. Dragon spotters should therefore protect themselves by wearing heavy lead-lined clothing and protective goggles, whenever Knucker watching.

## 5  Key features of a non-chronological report

Read the checklist. Make sure your writing has all the key features of a non-chronological report.

**Introduction often includes:**

An opening with a general classification using technical language, e.g. *Knucker dragons are a carnivorous dragon found in China.*

**Organisation of information can include:**

★ Tables, diagrams and pictures with captions to add interest.

★ Paragraphs with sub-headings (sometimes as questions).

★ Fact files, and short factual sentences organised by bullet points.

**Language features include:**

★ third person, present tense, for example: *These squid live…*

★ focus on generic subjects: *ogres, dragons, scientists*

★ descriptive language for precise, accurate descriptions

★ causal connectives: *this is because, therefore, however, so.*

### Challenge

A bestiary is an encyclopaedia that describes both real and imaginary animals. Find out more about bestiaries, and what kinds of animals can be found in them.

# Unit 6 Father's Day

## READING

**❶ Script version 3**
*TTYP*

**Discuss the questions below with your partner.**

**A.** What would you say to Cameron if you met him?

**B.** How well do you think Ria and Cameron get on?

**C.** Why did Cameron want to hurt Ria?

**D.** What did you think was going to happen at the end?

## ❷ Word power 2
*TTYP*

**Partner 1 read the word and its meaning.**
**Partner 2 read the sentences containing the word.**

★ *malicious* – spiteful, unkind

That was a *malicious* trick to play on your friend!

★ *eccentricities* – strangeness, weirdness, odd behaviour

I have got used to your *eccentricities*.

★ *quaint* – charming, pretty, old fashioned

My gran has lots of *quaint* china ornaments.

★ *devious* – sneaky, deceitful, crafty

My sister was very *devious*. She stole a biscuit when my mother briefly left the room.

★ *iridescent* – shimmering, shining, glistening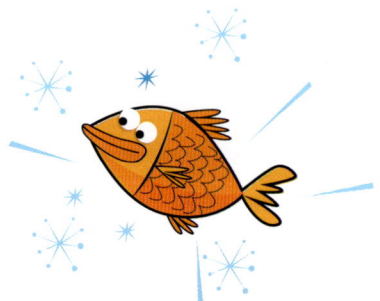

The fish's skin was *iridescent*.

## ❸ What's explicit, what's implicit? TTYP

**Discuss each question below with your partner. Give evidence to support all your answers.**

**Decide:**

★ Is the information you need *explicit* – can the answer to the question be found written down in the text?

★ Is the information you need *implicit* – will you have to work harder to answer this because the answer is not written down, it is hidden in the sub-text?

**A.** What did Ria say is 'against the law'?

**B.** Why did Cameron buy the kingfisher plate?

**C.** What does Lorraine feel about the family?

**D.** Why doesn't Ria see her dad very often?

**E.** Who is the easiest person to get on with in the family?

## 4  What if not...?  TTYP

**Discuss these What if not...? questions.**

**A.** What if not *humorous*? What if Steve was *grumpy*?

**B.** What if not *the same age*? What if Cameron was a lot *younger* than Ria?

**C.** What if not *just the two step-children*? What if Lorraine *had two children of her own* (so Ria had a brother or sister)?

**D.** What if not *the change of heart by Cameron*? What if Cameron *had given Steve the kingfisher plate himself*?

### Challenge

Draw a mind map showing the personalities and family relationships in the play *Father's Day*.

## 5  Dramatic improvisation  TTYP

**Partner 1: you are the TV interviewer and these are your questions:**

**A.** What was the worst thing about having a camera crew in the house for 12 weeks?

**B.** Whose behaviour in the family changed the most because of the cameras?

**Partner 2: you are either the boy or the girl from the Green family who starred in the documentary. Make up answers to the questions.**

**Now swap roles!**

**Partner 2: you are the TV interviewer and these are your questions:**

**C.** Do you think the public saw your family as it really is?

**D.** What is it like being recognised by people in the street?

**Partner 1: you are either the boy or the girl from the Green family who starred in the fly on the wall documentary. Make up answers to the questions.**

**Look at the questions together before you start and TTYP to share ideas for answers.**

## Challenge

If you could be a 'fly on the wall', where would you like to be? What would you like to observe unnoticed? Why?

Do you think it would really be possible to 'forget' that you are being filmed by a camera crew?

Think about these questions and write your thoughts in note form in your Daily log.

# WRITING

## 1 Show, don't tell

Build up this sentence into two or three 'showing' sentences using these prompt questions to help you.

*He went up to the young children playing in the park and told them to give him their football.*

**A.** What does he do with his chest and shoulders?

**B.** What about his hands?

**C.** How is he standing? Where is standing?

**D.** What does his mouth look like? What do his eyes look like?

### Challenge

Think of a list of words to describe the behaviour of bullies and another list of words to describe how a person being bullied might feel.

## 2 Evaluation TTYP

Take turns to read each section of 'Build a script 3' from your printout with your partner. Use the guide questions to help you to discuss the script.

**A.** Do you think the script was entertaining? If yes, why? If no, why not?

**B.** Which character would you like most of all as a friend? Why?

**C.** Which parts of the play made you feel sad? How?

**D.** Which stage directions were the most important?

### Challenge

You are an actor. Write three sentences explaining which role in the bully play you would audition for.

Use the prompts to help you build up the script below and add stage directions.

[Add stage direction here to describe the officer's actions]

**PCSO:** What does this bully boy look like then?

[Add stage direction here to describe Tommy's actions]

**Tommy:** Big and scary.

**Prompts**

**Remember to:**

★ Think of the more formal words the officer might use, e.g.

  *details, description, information, incident, statement*

★ Think of adjectives Tommy could use to describe the incident, e.g.

  It was really *terrifying, frightening*

★ Think about using exaggeration for comic effect, e.g.

  Tommy and Ben could start to *exaggerate* how big, threatening and scary the bully was! Katy might disagree with them.

**Say your speech out loud to your partner before writing it down. Make changes to it until you are really happy with it.**

**Challenge**

Design or describe costumes and props for the characters in the bully play. Think carefully about what their clothes could show us about their characters.

# Unit 6 Discussion texts

## READING AND WRITING

### 1 Word power TTYP

Partner 1 read the word and its meaning.
Partner 2 read the sentence containing the word.

★ *discuss* – talk about, argue, debate

Let's *discuss* where to go on holiday this year.

★ *persuade* – convince, influence, win over

I tried to *persuade* Mum to let me have a sleepover!

★ *balanced* – fair, presenting different sides of an argument, weighing for and against

I need a *balanced* view of the situation before I make up my mind!

★ *biased* – not a balanced point of view, one-sided

You say your team is the best but you are *biased*!

★ *personal* – individual, your own

You can take your *personal* belongings with you.

★ *impersonal* – neutral, unbiased

The news is read in an *impersonal* way by the presenter.

### 2 Balance and bias TTYP

With your partner, read texts A, B and C on the next page. Discuss what the main *issue* is in each text and prepare to feed back with examples to support your answers.

## A Blog

Dolphins are my favourite creatures! They are much more interesting than other mammals and deserve to be treated with respect as they are so intelligent. They are beautiful and if I had my way, everyone would sponsor one. How cool would that be? It is a disgrace to keep them in captivity, when they are an endangered species – they should be left in the wild. There is no reason to keep them in an aquarium!

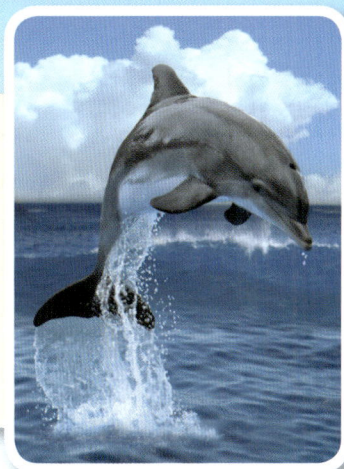

## B Letter to local newspaper

Dear Sir,

Dogs should be banned from public parks! They frighten little children, run after joggers and generally annoy people who are just trying to relax.

I know that some people think that a dog is a best friend. Well, how many best friends do you know who need a lead to keep them under control?

Yes, yes, dogs can be great company for the lonely and the elderly but so can a TV set (and you don't have to feed a TV set)!

## C Article in a magazine

Many people believe it is wrong to keep animals in captivity. However, others point out that there are good reasons for doing so.

It could be said that all wild creatures should be left to live freely in their natural habitat. On the other hand, it might be argued that it is in the wild that many animals face their biggest threat from humans, as they suffer from polluted seas, destruction of the rainforests and hunters.

*Deforestation leaves many wild animals without a home.*

### Challenge

Do some research and create a short PowerPoint presentation about *one* of the issues raised in texts A, B or C. Ask if you can show it to the class.

Use the following prompts to guide you when writing your own discussion text.

★ Use your planning grid to help you.

★ Say your first sentence to your partner before writing.

★ Read each sentence as soon as you have written in down, to check it makes sense.

★ Start a new paragraph for each new argument.

### Challenge

Think of an issue that people have strong views about. Make up a questionnaire to find out people's opinions on the issue in your school. It could be about anything from animals in circuses to children being given the right to vote at elections! Ask adults as well as children.